Central Texas Wildflowers

A My First Field Guide Book

By E. L. Botha

Key Vocabulary:

Annual: a plant with a one year life cycle

Biennial: a plant that completes its life cycle over two years, typically waiting until its second year to grow flowers or fruit

Perrenial: a plant with a life cycle that is longer than two years

Bract: a modified, or specialized leaf, usually found at the base of a flower

Parasitic: an organism that lives on and receives its nutrients from another organism

Think conservation first! If a population of plants is small, please refrain from collecting seeds or picking flowers. Remember, you may not collect flowers or seeds in National Parks.

Texas Bluebonnet
Lupinus texensis

8-16"; full sun; annual; well-drained sandy soil; fuzzy seed pods when done blooming

Texas bluebonnets bloom in March and April. Its blue blossoms are found in Texas, Oklahoma, Louisiana, and Florida; though it is most common in Central Texas. It is an annual and grows in open fields and along roadsides.

The bluebonnet is the state flower of Texas. There are five varieties of bluebonnet, but the Texas bluebonnet is the most commonly recognized of these.

Texas Indian Paintbrush
Castilleja indivisa

6-16" with flowers in 3" spikes; full sun; annual or biennial; sandy soil; seeds in capsules at the base of each flower. Collect when dry and brown

Texas Indian paintbrushes bloom from March to May and are found throughout Texas. They grow in open fields and along roadsides, often alongside other flowers. The flowers of the Texas Indian paintbrush are small and green, but are surrounded by bright reddish-orange bracts, or leaves.

The Texas Indian paintbrush is a parasitic plant. It reaches out with its roots until it penetrates the roots of other flowers or grasses to obtain nutrients. Depending upon growing conditions, it can be either an annual or biennial plant.

Mexican Hat
Ratibida columnifera

12-36"; full sun; perennial; well-drained soil; seeds are in the center of the flower, on the crown of the "hat". Can be collected when brown and dry

Mexican hats bloom from March to July and are found throughout Texas. They are common along roadsides and in fields. The petals are brown and yellow. The Mexican hat is part of the sunflower family. They are also called coneflowers or thimbleflowers.

The Mexican hat prefers hot, dry climates, is extremely drought tolerant, and can grow in a variety of soils. It is deer resistant and a good source of nectar for insects.

Firewheel
Gaillardia pulchella

12-24"; sun or partial shade; annual; well-drained soil; seeds are in the center of the flower. Collect after the petals have fallen off the flower and the seeds are dry and fluffy.

Firewheels bloom from March through July and are found throughout Texas. They are common along roadsides and in fields. The firewheel has red petals with yellow tips. It is also called Indian blanket.

The firewheel does well in hot, dry climates and is very drought tolerant. It is deer resistant.

Drummond's Phlox
Phlox drummondii

6-12"; full sun; well-drained soil; annual; seeds in capsules. When capsules change from green to light brown, collect seeds from them

Drummond's phlox blooms from March to June. They are native to Texas and can be found in grasslands and open woodlands. Drummond's phlox can be found in many colors, including red, purple, pink, and white.

The Drummond phlox get their name from botanist Thomas Drummond, who collected their seeds and sent them back to England in 1835. Since then, phlox have been a highly valued ornamental flower in Europe, where they have bred around two hundred different color varieties.

Winecup
Callirhoe digitata

8-20"; full sun; perennial; dry and rocky soils; collect seeds when flowers are done blooming

Winecups bloom from April to August. They are found throughout Texas in prairies, open woods, or grassy slopes. The blooms are violet in color and have five petals. The petals are in the shape of a cup when they first bloom, and flatten out as they mature.

Winecups are also known as poppy mallow and buffalo rose. They are extremely drought tolerant and will bloom again in fall if dead blossoms are trimmed back.

Wild Onion
Allium drummondii

10-12" with 4" ball of blossoms; full sun; perennial; well-drained soil; collect seeds late May/early June

Wild onion, also known as wild garlic, blooms from March through May. It can be found in the Midwest from Texas to South Dakota in meadows and plains. Its white and pink flowers grow in clusters on top of a long, thin stem.

Wild Onion is edible, but must be cooked for a long time before they are digestible. Native Americans frequently used wild onion while cooking.

Mealy Blue Sage
Salvia farinacea

2-3' tall and wide; full sun; perennial; well-drained limestone or sandy soil; collect seeds when capsules begin to dry out, but before they drop from plant

Mealy blue sage blooms from April to October. It can be found in prairies, meadows, and along woodland edges in Texas and New Mexico. It's flowers are blue and grow on the end of purple-blue or light blue stalks.

Mealy blue sage grows in a mound that is typically as wide as it is high. It attracts both butterflies and hummingbirds.

Pink Evening Primrose
Oenothera speciosa

1-2'; full sun; perennial; well-drained soil of various types; 4 seed capsules replace flowers

Pink evening primrose blooms from February through July. It grows throughout the United States except in the northernmost portions. It can be found in open grasslands, hillsides, and fields. Its pink or white flowers have four petals that are lined with dark pink, or red veins. It often grows in large colonies.

Many pink evening primroses open their blossoms in the evening, and close them in the morning. However, in the southern part of their range, they do the opposite; opening in the morning and closing in the evening.

Scarlet Beeblossom
Guara coccinea

1-2'; full-sun; perennial; dry, sandy soil; no seeds, but can grow new plants with cuttings or by dividing adult plants

The scarlet beeblossom blooms from May through August. It is native to most of the Untied States and can be found almost everywhere but the north- and southeast. It grows on prairies and roadsides. Its pink and white flowers grow on a stalk starting at the bottom and making their way to the top.

Each flower blooms for only one day. It starts out white, then turns pink, and finally red, all on the same day. One ring of flowers blooms on each stalk at a time. The blooming flowers work their way up the stalk each day.

Dear Readers,

I hope you and your little ones have enjoyed Central Texas Wildflowers! You can follow me at http://www.facebook.com/elbothaauthor or visit my website http://elbotha.com to check out my other works. You can also subscribe to my monthly newsletter from my website. I promise to send you updates, giveaways, and activities for you and your little ones; never spam!

Thank you and happy reading!

E. L. Botha

Other Books by E. L. Botha:

The Volcano Dragon Series:

The Volcano Dragon

The Volcano Dragon Saves the Day

My First Field Guide Series:

Little Ornithologist

Little Lepidopterist

Little Ophiologist

Little Backyard Naturalist

Central Texas Wildflowers

Made in the USA
Charleston, SC
16 November 2016